30 Days Ramadan Mubarak Meal Plans

Effortless Eats for Iftar & Suhoor: Your 30-Day Ramadan Cookbook

+Bonus 28-Day Ramadan Meal Plan Table.

Paperback only (Page 66)

MELVIN A. ORR

1

Gratitude

As Salam Alaikum (Peace be upon you), Dear Reader,

As we dig in this Ramadan recipes cookbook, I want to use this moment to express my heartfelt gratitude for you taking out of your time to purchase this cookbook as your companion guide throughout your Ramadan journey.

May the meals you prepare from these pages nourish your body and soul, and may they bring joy and togetherness to your table as you break your fast each evening. Enjoy!

Table of Contents:

INTRODUCTION

Ramadan Mubarak! As the crescent moon graces the night sky, ushering in the holy month of Ramadan, Muslims worldwide embark on a spiritual journey of fasting, prayer, and charity. It's a time for self-reflection, heightened devotion, and strengthening our connection with Allah (SWT). This Ramadan, embark on a delicious and nourishing adventure alongside your faith-based practice. "**30 Days Ramadan Mubarak Meal Plans**" is your comprehensive guide to crafting a balanced and fulfilling menu for the entire month.

A short scenario between me and one of my neighbors named Aminat;

Amina stared at the fridge, its emptiness echoing the hollowness in her stomach. It was Ramadan, and after a long day of work, the thought of preparing a feast for the iftar felt daunting. Just then, she spotted her new Ramadan recipe cookbook. Flipping through colorful pages filled with quick suhoor and iftar ideas, a wave of relief washed over her.

She found a recipe for lentil soup – perfect for a light suhoor. The instructions were clear and concise, and with a few pantry staples, she had a nourishing meal ready in minutes. That night, she browsed the iftar section, drawn to vibrant pictures of spiced lamb kebabs. The recipe was surprisingly simple, using pre-marinated meat for a burst of flavor.

Over the next few days, the cookbook became Amina's Ramadan companion. She discovered hidden gems – creamy eggplant moussaka for suhoor, and fragrant chicken tagine for iftar. Each dish was not only delicious but also surprisingly quick to prepare. Amina realized the cookbook wasn't just saving time, it was saving her energy – a precious commodity during the fast.

The best part? Ramadan became less about the stress of cooking and more about the joy of sharing meals with loved ones. Amina felt a newfound appreciation for the cookbook, a testament to the power of simple recipes that nourish both the body and the soul.
We understand the importance of maintaining physical and spiritual well-being throughout the extended fasting hours. This book offers a meticulously crafted roadmap to ensure your pre-dawn Suhoor and post-dusk Iftar meals provide the necessary energy, essential nutrients, and delightful flavors to sustain you throughout the holy month. Within these pages, you'll discover not just an array of delectable recipes, but a treasure trove of practical guidance.

It will equip you with planning and preparation strategies to streamline your Ramadan cooking, suggest a well-stocked pantry list to avoid last-minute dashes to the store, and provide clever hydration hacks to keep you feeling your best. As you navigate the 30 days of Ramadan, this book will be your trusted companion. It will inspire you with recipe suggestions for each day, while also offering customization tips to cater to your preferences and dietary needs.

Let's embark on this Ramadan together.

DELICIOUS SUHOOR AND IFTAR RECIPES

SUHOOR RECIPES:

As the sacred month of Ramadan unfolds, Muslims around the world embark on a spiritual trip marked by dieting from dawn to dusk. Suhoor, the pre-dawn menu, plays a vital role in sustaining individuals throughout the day, providing the energy needed to endure the fast until iftar.   Beyond its functional significance, Suhoor is an opportunity to indulge in wholesome, nutritious, and delicious dishes that not only nourish the body but also delight the taste buds before the sun rises.

Spinach Tofu Scramble:

This quick and nourishing Spinach Tofu Scramble suits any meal, not just breakfast. It calls for spinach, but add any veggies and power up with plant-based protein!

PREP TIME: 7 mins

COOK TIME: 8 mins

TOTAL TIME: 15 mins

SERVINGS: 3

Ingredients

- 1 tablespoon extra virgin olive oil
- ½ (about ½ cup) yellow onion, diced
- 1 pound firm or extra firm tofu packed in water, drained well
- 1 teaspoon nutritional yeast
- ½ teaspoon kosher salt, plus more to taste
- ¼ teaspoon freshly ground black pepper, plus more to taste
- ¼ teaspoon ground turmeric
- 4 cups loosely packed fresh spinach leaves
- ¼ teaspoon lemon juice

Directions

> Cook the onion:

Heat a medium skillet over medium-high heat. Add oil; when it ripples, add the onion. Cook, stirring occasionally, until the onion is soft, 3 to 5 minutes.

> Add the tofu and seasonings:

Use your fingers to crumble the drained tofu into bite-sized pieces. You can do this directly over the skillet.

Add the nutritional yeast, salt, pepper, and turmeric, and stir to combine. Cook, stirring occasionally, until the tofu is hot, about 3 minutes. You're not aiming to brown the tofu here, but if that happens a little, it's not an issue.

> Add the spinach, wilt, and finish with lemon juice:

Add the spinach and cook until wilted, 1 minute. Sprinkle the lemon juice over the scramble. Taste and adjust the seasoning with salt and pepper, if needed. Leftover tofu scramble will be kept in a tightly covered container for up to four days. I don't recommend freezing it.

CALORIES: 241

FAT: 13g

CARBS: 15g

PROTEIN: 23g

Zucchini Tomato Quiche:

Make the best of the summer's bounty with this zucchini tomato quiche. With freshly grated zucchini, colorful cherry tomatoes, basil, and Parmesan, it's just the thing for brunch, or a make-ahead breakfast or lunch.

PREP TIME: 7 mins

COOK TIME: 8 mins

TOTAL TIME: 15 mins

SERVINGS: 3

Ingredients

For the crust:

- 1 recipe for all butter crust pie dough, rolled out and lining a 9 or 10-inch pie plate, frozen for at least 30 minutes

For the filling:

- 1/2-pound zucchini (about 1 1/2 cups shredded)
- 2 tablespoons extra virgin olive oil
- 1 cup sliced shallots or spring onions
- 4 large eggs, room temperature
- 1/2 cup milk
- 1/3 cup cream
- 1/3 cup sour cream
- 1 teaspoon dried herbs de Provence (can substitute Italian herb blend)
- 10 basil leaves, sliced
- 1 tablespoon chopped fresh parsley
- 1/2 teaspoon salt
- 1/2 teaspoon black pepper
- 1 cup (3 ounces) packed, shredded Parmesan cheese
- 10 cherry tomatoes, halved or quartered

Direction

- Pre-bake the crust:

Heat oven to 350°F. If using a homemade pie crust, freeze it for at least 30 minutes.

Line the inside of the crust with heavy-duty aluminum foil. Fill the pie crust to the top with pie weights—either sugar, dry rice, or dry beans. (I prefer to use sugar).

Bake for 50 minutes. Remove from oven, remove foil and pie weights from the crust.

Note: If you're using a store-bought crust, you can defrost it and skip the pre-baking, or partially pre-bake it using the instructions for pre-baking on the package.

➢ Prep the zucchini:

Grate the zucchini using the large holes of a box grater. Set the grated zucchini in a mesh sieve set over a bowl to drain off excess moisture.

➢ Cook the shallots:

Heat olive oil in a skillet on medium heat. Add the sliced shallots or spring onions and toss to coat with the oil. Lower the heat to low and cook gently for several minutes, occasionally stirring.

Once softened and lightly browned, remove from heat.

➢ Make the filling:

Beat the eggs in a large bowl. Whisk in the milk, cream, and sour cream. Whisk in the dried herbs de Provence, the fresh sliced basil leaves, chopped parsley, salt, and pepper.

Stir in the grated Parmesan cheese and the grated zucchini.

➢ Assemble the quiche:

Spread cooked shallots over the bottom of the pre-baked shell. Pour the zucchini filling mixture on top. Arrange cut cherry tomatoes on the top of the filling, pushing each one in about halfway.

➢ Bake:

Bake for 45 to 55 minutes at 350°F, until set in the center. If the edges of the crust look like they might get too browned, tent them with foil or a pie protector. Note that if you are using a store-bought crust that is shallower than a homemade crust, the quiche will cook more quickly.

Remove from oven when the center of the quiche has set and the top is lightly browned.

Let it cool completely before serving.

CALORIES: 421

FAT: 27g

CARBS: 34g

PROTEIN: 11g

They are desserts in the morning, only healthy and perfect for those who have a busy morning schedule or are looking for a nutritious Suhoor meal during Ramadan.

PREP TIME: 5 mins

SOAKING TIME: 8 hrs

TOTAL TIME: 8 hrs 5 mins

SERVINGS: 2

Ingredients

- 1/2 cup old-fashioned oats
- 1/2 cup buttermilk
- 1/2 teaspoon vanilla or almond extract
- 1/2 cup plain yogurt
- 1/2 cup strawberries
- 2 to 3 teaspoons honey
- 1 tablespoon toasted slivered almonds (optional)

Directions

- Soak the oats and prepare the strawberries:

In a small bowl, combine old-fashioned oats, buttermilk, and extract. In a separate small bowl, combine honey and sliced strawberries. Stir to combine.

➢ Refrigerate overnight:

Cover the bowls and place in the fridge to soften overnight. Oatmeal cups can also be prepped and kept refrigerated up to 5 days in advance.

➢ Add the yogurt and berries:

In the morning, the oats should look thick and creamy. Top with yogurt, and spoon the strawberries and any juice that they've released over the yogurt. Sprinkle with almonds. Eat!

Alternative instructions: Combine everything except the almonds in a pint-size jar. Stir to combine. Place in fridge overnight or for up to 5 days. Top with almonds. Eat.

CALORIES: 372

FAT: 6g

CARBS: 66g

PROTEIN: 16g

Breakfast Wraps with Spinach and Feta:

Make-ahead feta and spinach breakfast wraps make life easy during this Ramadan! Great for weekend brunches or breakfast during the week.

PREP TIME: 15 mins

COOK TIME: 35 mins

TOTAL TIME: 50 mins

SERVINGS: 4-8

Ingredients

- ➢ 2 tablespoons olive oil
- ➢ 4 scallions, thinly sliced
- ➢ 1 teaspoon dried oregano
- ➢ 8 large eggs, well beaten
- ➢ Kosher salt and freshly ground black pepper
- ➢ 4 (10-inch) flour tortillas
- ➢ 3 ounces (about 3 cups packed) fresh baby spinach leaves
- ➢ 1/2 cup (4 ounces) crumbled feta cheese

Directions

- ➢ Prepare the parchment paper:

Cut four 12-inch squares of parchment paper and set them nearby.

- ➢ Scramble the eggs:

In a large nonstick skillet over medium heat, heat the oil. Add the scallions and oregano and cook for 2 to 3 minutes, or until the scallions soften slightly.

Add the eggs, salt, and pepper, and cook, stirring constantly, until starting to set but still runny.

- ➢ Add the spinach:

Take the pan off the heat and fold in the spinach. Turn the heat to medium-low, and return the pan to heat. Continue to cook for 1 to 3 minutes longer, or until the spinach starts to wilt (some leaves will still be un-wilted) and the eggs are cooked.

Transfer the eggs to a platter to cool slightly. Wash out the skillet.

- ➢ Warm the tortillas:

Place the cleaned skillet over medium heat, and heat until hot. One at a time, warm the tortillas for 15 to 20 seconds on a side, turning with tongs, until softened and lightly browned in spots, but not crisp. Stack on a plate and cover with a tea towel to keep warm and pliable.

- ➢ Make the wraps:

Spread a quarter of the egg filling in a line about 2 inches from the bottom edge of a tortilla. Sprinkle with 2 tablespoons of feta.

Fold the bottom edge of the tortilla over the filling. Fold in the sides and roll to enclose the filling in a neat bundle. With the seam side down, wrap in the parchment paper. Repeat with the remaining tortillas and filling.

Store the wraps in the refrigerator until ready to serve.

➢ Preheat the oven:

Preheat the oven to 350°F.

➢ Reheat:

Place the wraps on their parchment paper in a baking dish and warm for 15 to 20 minutes, or until hot. Remove from the oven and remove the paper. (Alternatively, warm individual wraps in the microwave, but the oven is better for reheating several at once.)

Cut each wrap in half on the diagonal and serve.

CALORIES: 257

FAT: 14g

CARBS: 21g

PROTEIN: 13g

Note: You may quadruple this recipe, but you'll have to work in batches or use a bigger skillet for cooking the eggs. You can prepare and store these wraps in the refrigerator for up to two days. Before serving, reheat for a little while in the oven or microwave.

You may freeze the wraps as well. Place them on a small pan and freeze until solid, first wrapping them in parchment paper and then foil. Put them in a freezer bag made of polypropylene. Use the microwave to reheat.

Jamaican Goat Curry:

Jamaican Curry Goat – insanely delicious slow-cooked Jamaican Spiced Curry that is full of flavor and tender to the bone! A must-make Jamaican food! So easy to make with minimal prep.

PREP TIME: 15 mins

COOK TIME: 2 hrs 30 mins

TOTAL TIME: 2 hrs 45 mins

SERVINGS: 6-8

Ingredients

- 1/4 cup vegetable oil
- 6 to 8 tablespoons curry powder
- 1 tablespoon allspice (see Step 1)
- 3 pounds goat stew meat (use lamb or beef if you can't find goat)
- Salt
- 2 medium onions, chopped
- 1 to 2 habanero or Scotch bonnet peppers, seeded and chopped
- 1 (2-inch) piece ginger, peeled and minced
- 1 head garlic, peeled and chopped
- 1 to 2 (15-ounce) cans of coconut milk
- 1 (15-ounce) can of tomato sauce or crushed tomatoes
- 1 tablespoon dried thyme
- 3 to 4 cups water
- 5 Yukon gold potatoes, peeled and cut into 1-inch chunks

Directions

- Make the curry powder:

If you can find Jamaican curry powder, definitely use it. If not, use regular curry powder and add the allspice to it. You will need at least 6 tablespoons of spices for this stew, and you can kick it up to 8-9 depending on how spicy you like it.

- Cut and salt the goat meat:

Cut the meat into large chunks, maybe 2-3 inches across. If you have bones, you can use them, too. Salt everything well and set aside to come to room temperature for about 30 minutes.

➤ Heat the curry powder in oil:

Heat the oil in a large pot over medium-high heat. Mix in 2 tablespoons of the curry powder and heat until fragrant.

➤ Brown meat in curried oil:

Pat the meat dry and brown well in the curried oil. Do this in batches and don't overcrowd the pot. It will take a while to do this, maybe 30 minutes or so. Set the browned meat aside in a bowl. (When all the meat is browned, if you have bones, add them and brown them, too.)

➤ Cook onions, habanero, ginger, garlic:

Add the onions and habanero to the pot and sauté, stirring from time to time, until the onions just start to brown, about 5 minutes. Sprinkle some salt over them as they cook. Add the ginger and garlic, mix well, and sauté for another 1-2 minutes.

Put the meat (and bones, if using) back into the pot, along with any juices left in the bowl. Mix well.

➤ Add coconut milk, tomatoes, curry powder, water, thyme, then simmer:

Pour in the coconut milk and tomatoes and 5 tablespoons of the curry powder. Stir to combine. If you are using 2 cans of coconut milk, add 3 cups of water. If you're only using 1 can, add 4 cups of water. Add the thyme.

Bring to a simmer and let it cook until the meat is falling apart tender, which will take at least 2 hours. Longer if you have a mature goat.

➤ Add potatoes:

Once the meat is close to being done – tender but not falling apart yet – Add the potatoes and mix in. The stew is done when the potatoes are. Taste for salt and add some if it needs it.

➤ Skim fat:

You might need to skim off the layer of fat at the top of the curry before serving. Do this with a large, shallow spoon, skimming into a bowl. Also, be sure to remove any bones before you serve the curry.

The stew is better the day after, or even several days after, the day you make it.

Serve with Jamaican rice and peas, a coconut rice with kidney beans.

CALORIES: 459

FAT: 24g

CARBS: 28g

PROTEIN: 36g

Egg Bites:

If you are searching for a quick, easy, and delicious on-the-go breakfast, then these Instant Pot egg bites are for you! They are simple to whip up and are easy to store in the fridge for the week to keep your body fueled until sunset.

PREP TIME: 10 mins

COOK TIME: 25 mins

TOTAL TIME: 35 mins

SERVINGS: 7

Ingredients

- 3 large eggs
- 1/4 cup cottage cheese
- 1/4 cup soft cheese, like cream cheese, Brie, Boursin, or Laughing Cow
- 1/2 cup chopped mix-ins, like cooked meats and/or raw or cooked vegetables
- 1/2 cup shredded cheese, such as cheddar, Monterey Jack, or mozzarella

Directions

- Blend the eggs and cheeses:

Combine the eggs, cottage cheese, and soft cheese in a blender. Blend at medium speed for about 30 seconds, until smooth.

> ➢ Add the mix-ins:

Pour the blended egg mixture into a bowl. Add the chopped mix-ins and shredded cheese and stir to combine.

> ➢ Fill the molds:

Use a small amount of oil or nonstick cooking spray to grease a silicone egg mold, then ladle 1/4 cup of the mixture into each of the impressions in the mold. Wipe off any drips.

> ➢ Prepare the pressure cooker:

Pour 1 cup of water into the Instant Pot or electric pressure cooker. Carefully transfer the egg mold to the wire steam rack, then place an 8-inch parchment round or piece of aluminum foil on top of the mold to keep condensation from dripping onto the bites as they cook.

Grasping the handles of the steam rack, lower the egg mold into the pot.

> ➢ Cook the eggs on low pressure:

Secure the lid on the pressure cooker. Make sure that the pressure regulator is set to the "Sealing" position. Select the "Pressure Cook" or "Manual" program, then adjust the time to 8 minutes at low pressure.

(If making a double batch, increase the cooking time to 10 minutes.)

The pressure cooker will take about 10 minutes to come up to full pressure. Cook time begins once it has reached full pressure.

Note: If you don't have a low-pressure option on your pressure cooker, use the 'Pressure Cook' or 'Manual' setting for 8 minutes. We recommend only doing one layer of egg bites at a time this way. You can also try setting the "Steam" function for 10 minutes.

> ➢ Release the pressure naturally for 5 minutes:

When the timer goes off, let the pressure release naturally for 5 minutes, then perform a quick pressure release by moving the pressure release knob from "Sealing" to "Venting." It will take a minute or two for the pressure to release completely.

> ➢ Remove the egg bites from the pressure cooker:

Wearing heatproof mitts, grasp the ends of the wire rack to lift the egg bite mold out of the pot. Remove the sheet of parchment and let the bites cool for 2 minutes or so (they will deflate a bit as they cool). Use a spoon to scoop the bites out of the mold and transfer them to a serving dish.

> ➢ Serve the egg bites:

Serve the bites warm on their own, or with toast or a pile of mixed greens.

You can refrigerate them for up to 3 days in a tightly lidded container. To reheat, microwave very briefly (about 25 seconds, depending on the strength of your microwave), before serving.

CALORIES: 221

FAT: 9g

CARBS: 1g

PROTEIN: 9g

Quick and Easy Green Smoothie:

This healthy green smoothie helps you get your greens during your daily schedules before Iftar.

PREP TIME: 5 mins

TOTAL TIME: 5 mins

SERVINGS: 2

Ingredients

> ➢ 1 medium ripe banana
> ➢ 1 cup of fresh, canned, or frozen pineapple
> ➢ 3 large handfuls of fresh spinach (washed)
> ➢ 1 cup of plain Greek yogurt

➢ 6 oz. water

Directions

➢ Combine the ingredients:

Into a blender add the banana, pineapple, spinach, Greek yogurt, and water. Blend until smooth. Enjoy!

Note: If you use canned pineapple, you can add the juice, too, for a sweeter-tasting smoothie.

Mango Lassi:

Mango Lassi is a popular dessert drink from the Indian Sub-continent and a summer special loved by everyone. Mangoes, yogurt, milk/cream, ground cardamoms, and a little sweetener will take you to mango heaven! This is perfect for hot days in Ramadan.

PREP TIME: 10 mins

TOTAL TIME: 10 mins

SERVINGS: 2

Ingredients

➢ 1 cup chopped very ripe mango (see how to peel and chop mango), frozen chopped mango, or canned mango pulp
➢ 1 cup plain yogurt
➢ 1/2 cup milk
➢ 4 teaspoons honey or sugar, more or less to taste
➢ Dash ground cardamom, optional
➢ Ice, optional

Directions

➢ Add the ingredients to the blender:

Put the mango, yogurt, milk, honey (or sugar), and cardamom (optional) into a blender and blend for 2 minutes.

If you want a thicker consistency, either blend in some ice as well or serve over ice cubes.

➢ Serve with a sprinkle of cardamom:

Pour contents into a glass and sprinkle with a tiny pinch of ground cardamom to serve.

The lassi can be kept refrigerated for up to 24 hours.

CALORIES: 195

FAT: 3g

CARBS: 35g

PROTEIN: 9g

Note: Depending on how ripe and sweet the mango that you are using is, or if you are using already canned and sweetened mango pulp, you will need to add more or less honey or sugar to the lassi.

If you have cardamom pods, crush the pods to remove the seeds, then grind the seeds with a mortar and pestle.

Chia Pudding with Blueberries and Almonds:

This Chia Pudding with Blueberries and Almonds is EASY to make, loaded with fiber, protein, and antioxidants, perfect for a healthy breakfast!

PREP TIME: 5 mins

COOK TIME: 2 hrs

TOTAL TIME: 2 hrs 5 mins

SERVINGS: 2-3

Ingredients

- 2 cups unsweetened almond milk
- 1 cup (divided, 3/4 cup and 1/4 cup) fresh or frozen (defrosted) blueberries
- 1/2 cup chia seeds
- 2 tablespoons honey (optional)
- 1/2 teaspoon ground cinnamon
- 1/2 teaspoon vanilla extract
- 1/4 cup toasted slivered or sliced almonds

Directions

- Blend 2 cups almond milk and 3/4 cup blueberries:

in a blender. Pour out into a bowl or quart-sized mason jar.

- Stir in the chia seeds, honey, cinnamon, vanilla extract:

(Or just cover and shake if using a jar.) Let sit for 10 minutes, then stir again to break up any clumping.

- Chill:

for 2 hours or overnight.

- When ready to eat, stir again. Top with toasted almonds and the remaining blueberries

CALORIES: 266

FAT: 16g

CARBS: 24g

PROTEIN: 9g

Sweet Potato and Black Bean Breakfast Burrito:

Sweet Potato and Black Bean Breakfast Burrito are a perfect make-ahead meal for busy mornings before any schedules during Ramadan.

PREP TIME: 5 mins

COOK TIME: 20 mins

TOTAL TIME: 25 mins

SERVINGS: 3-5

Ingredients

- 1 Yellow Onion, diced
- 3 Medium to Large Sweet Potatoes, peeled and diced
- 1 cup Black Beans (rinse and drain if using canned)
- 1 cup Salsa of choice
- 2 cup Fresh Spinach
- Wraps of Choice
- Optional: Parchment Paper, for wrapping

Directions

- Rinse, Peel, and Dice all veggies.
- Add 1/3 cup of water to a large saucepan or skillet and add the Diced Onion and Sweet Potatoes. Cover and let cook over medium-high heat for 5-7 minutes.
- Remove the lid from the pan, reduce the heat to medium, and add the Black Beans and Salsa. Add a splash of water as well, if necessary. Stir, cover, and

let cook for 10-15 minutes, or until the sweet potatoes are tender. Remove from heat and set aside.

- ➢ Once the Sweet Potato and Bean mixture is cool enough to handle, make your burritos using a Wrap of your choice. Add a small handful of fresh Spinach to each wrap, if desired. Wrap each burrito with parchment paper and store in the fridge for up to 6 days, or the freezer for up to 30.
- ➢ To reheat the burritos, simply microwave for 2-3 minutes until warm and thawed. Serve with additional salsa, guacamole, or hummus.

CALORIES: 398

FAT: 13g

CARBS: 54g

PROTEIN: 18g

Almond Butter Date Balls:

These almond butter date balls fit the ticket perfectly! It will keep you full without much effort till sunset (Iftar). Protein-packed, convenient, and easy to make. Plus, dates add a sweetness that kids (and adults) love!

PREP TIME: 5 mins

COOK TIME: 30 mins

TOTAL TIME: 35 mins

SERVINGS: 5-8

Ingredients

For the balls:

- ➢ 1/2 cup walnuts
- ➢ 1/2 cup pitted dates (about 4 to 5), cut into quarters
- ➢ 1/2 cup cocoa powder, any kind (I usually use Hershey's Special Dark)

- ➢ Scant 1/2 cup maple syrup
- ➢ 1/2 cup almond butter
- ➢ 1/2 teaspoon vanilla extract
- ➢ 1/4 teaspoon fine sea salt
- ➢ 1/2 cup whole almonds
- ➢ Cooking spray, optional

For the topping:

- ➢ 1/2 cup unsweetened shredded coconut
- ➢ 1/2 cup cocoa powder

Special Equipment:

- ➢ Food Processor

Directions

- ➢ Start the date balls:

Place the walnuts and dates into the bowl of a food processor fitted with the blade, and pulse several times until well combined. The pieces should look like a rough crumble.

Add the cocoa powder, maple syrup, almond butter, vanilla extract, and sea salt and pulse until the mixture is smooth and thick; it will start to peel away from the edge of the bowl.

When this happens, stop the food processor; if it keeps whirring away, it may get stuck because these ingredients are, well, sticky! Keep a close eye on this, as it will come together quickly.

- ➢ Add the almonds:

Add the almonds and pulse a few times to incorporate them. You want them sort of irregularly sized so that some pieces are still pretty crunchy and offer a variety of textures.

- ➢ Roll the date balls:

Line a rimmed baking sheet with parchment or wax paper. Place the coconut in a small bowl and the cocoa powder in another bowl.

Using a cookie scoop measuring about 1 1/2 tablespoons (like this one) and sprayed with cooking spray for easy release, scoop out the mixture, roll it into golf-ball shapes, and roll in the shredded coconut or the cocoa powder. (I usually do some in coconut and some in cocoa powder, and leave some plain.)

> ➢ Chill and store the date balls:

Transfer the date balls to the baking sheet and chill them for a few hours or overnight, if needed. Once they've firmed up, transfer them to a plastic-lidded container and keep them in the fridge for several weeks, but I've never, ever, had them last that long. They are usually consumed too quickly.

CALORIES: 169

FAT: 11g

CARBS: 17g

PROTEIN: 4g

Protein-Packed Cottage Cheese Parfait:

Enjoy a delicious protein-packed parfait with fresh blueberries and Hood Maple and Vanilla Cottage Cheese for breakfast to get your day started or as a snack throughout the day before Iftar!

PREP TIME: 5 mins

TOTAL TIME: 5 mins

SERVINGS: 1-2

Ingredients

> ➢ 1 cup cottage cheese I recommend full-fat
> ➢ 2-3 tablespoons honey
> ➢ 1 teaspoon vanilla extract

- ➢ 1 tablespoon nut butter of choice you can omit if you are allergic but this adds creaminess
- ➢ + ~¼ cup fruit of choice
- ➢ +optional toppings of bee pollen and chocolate

Directions

- ➢ Add cottage cheese, honey, vanilla, and nut butter to a blender and blend until smooth.
- ➢ Layer cottage cheese with fruit, add desired toppings and dig in.

CALORIES: 345

FAT: 9g

CARBS: 42g

PROTEIN: 23g

Oat and Tahini Breakfast Cookies:

They are a healthy and delicious grab-and-go option for busy mornings. They complement a cup of tea or coffee, have little added sugar, and are gluten-free. Each cookie is chock full of nuts, dried fruit, and tahini!

PREP TIME: 15 mins

COOK TIME: 12 mins

TOTAL TIME: 27 mins

SERVINGS: 12

Note: You'll need a food processor for this.

Ingredients

- 1/4 cup pepitas
- 1/4 cup walnuts, coarsely chopped
- 1/4 cup whole almonds
- 1 1/2 cups old-fashioned rolled oats, divided
- 1/2 teaspoon baking powder
- 1/2 teaspoon salt
- 1/4 cup (4 tablespoons, 1/2 stick unsalted butter, at room temperature
- 1/4 cup brown sugar
- 1 large egg
- 1 large egg white
- 1/4 cup tahini
- 1 teaspoon vanilla
- 1 teaspoon finely grated orange zest
- 3/4 cup raisins, diced apricots, and/or cranberries, alone or in combination

Directions

- Preheat the oven to 375°F.

Set an oven rack in the middle position. Line a baking sheet with parchment.

- Toast the seeds and nuts:

On the baking sheet, spread the pumpkin seeds, walnuts, and almonds. Roast for 8 to 10 minutes, or until the nuts are fragrant. Let it cool briefly.

- Grind 1/2 cup of the oats:

In a food processor, finely grind 1/2 cup of the oats to make oat flour. Add the baking powder and salt and pulse to combine.

- Mix the dough:

In the bowl of a stand mixer fitted with the paddle attachment or by hand with a wooden spoon, beat the butter and sugar together until creamy. Add the egg, egg white, tahini, vanilla, and orange zest. Mix until combined, scraping down the bowl as needed.

Add the oat flour mixture to the dough and mix on low speed until blended.

Stir in oats, nuts, and dried fruit:

Add the remaining 1 cup of oats, pumpkin seeds, walnuts, almonds, and dried fruit, and stir to combine.

➢ Drop the cookies onto the baking sheet:

Use a cookie scoop or two spoons to drop the dough blobs (about a 1/4 cup each) onto the baking sheet, spacing them about 2 inches apart. Wet your fingers and gently press the dough to form 3-inch circles with a flat top.

➢ Bake the cookies:

Bake the cookies for 10 to 12 minutes, or until they are light brown. Remove from the oven and leave to cool completely on the baking sheet.

CALORIES: 204

FAT: 12g

CARBS: 21g

PROTEIN: 5g

Blueberry Peach Fruit Salad with Thyme:

Blueberry, peach, nectarine fruit salad seasoned with fresh thyme, ginger, and lemon juice.

PREP TIME: 15 mins

TOTAL TIME: 15 mins

SERVINGS: 4-8

Ingredients

➢ 4 peaches
➢ 4 nectarines
➢ 1 cup of blueberries
➢ 2 teaspoons of fresh, chopped thyme

- ➢ 1 teaspoon of grated ginger
- ➢ 1/4 cup of lemon juice
- ➢ 1 teaspoon of lemon zest
- ➢ 1/2 cup of water
- ➢ 1/4 cup of sugar (depending on how sweet the fruit is, you may be able to skip all altogether)
- ➢ Or 1 tablespoon of agave syrup instead of water and sugar

Directions

- ➢ Make simple syrup:

If using water and sugar place them into a saucepan and bring to a boil and the liquid is reduced by half into a simple syrup. Allow to cool.

- ➢ Combine ingredients:

Chop up the peaches and nectarines and place them in a bowl with the blueberries. Pour over the cooled simple syrup or agave syrup. Add the thyme, lemon juice, lemon zest, and ginger.

- ➢ Chill for 1 hour:

Stir and cover with plastic wrap, place in the fridge, and allow to macerate for one hour. Serve.

Baked Eggs in Avocado with Salmon:

Baked Eggs in Avocado might just be a healthy and nutritious Suhoor meal for your breakfast before sunset.

PREP TIME: 10 mins

COOK TIME: 20 mins

TOTAL TIME: 30 mins

SERVINGS: 4-6

Ingredients

For the everything bagel seasoning

- ➢ 2 tablespoons poppy seeds
- ➢ 1 tablespoon white sesame seeds
- ➢ 1 tablespoon black sesame seeds
- ➢ 1 tablespoon plus 1 teaspoon dried minced garlic
- ➢ 1 tablespoon plus 1 teaspoon dried minced onion
- ➢ 2 teaspoons flaked sea salt or coarse salt

For the baked eggs in avocado

- ➢ 3 large Haas avocados, halved and pitted
- ➢ 6 ounces smoked salmon or lox, thinly sliced
- ➢ 6 large eggs
- ➢ 1/2 teaspoon salt, divided
- ➢ 1/2 teaspoon freshly ground black pepper, divided
- ➢ 1/4 teaspoon red chili pepper flakes, divided
- ➢ 1/3 cup red onion, thinly sliced

For garnish

- ➢ 1/2 cup crumbled feta cheese
- ➢ 1 bunch fresh dill, chopped
- ➢ 3 tablespoons capers, drained
- ➢ Everything bagel seasoning
- ➢ Lemon wedges, garnish

Directions

- ➢ Preheat the oven and prepare a baking sheet:

Preheat the oven to 425°F. Lightly oil or spray a baking sheet with nonstick spray.

- ➢ Make the everything bagel seasoning:

In a small bowl, combine the poppy seeds, white sesame seeds, black sesame seeds, dried garlic, dried onion, and salt. Stir until well combined. Store in a sealed jar or container until ready to use.

> Prep the avocados

Using a spoon, scoop out about one tablespoon of avocado flesh, or more, as needed to enlarge the well in the center of each avocado. You want it to be wide. Arrange the avocado halves on a baking sheet and line the hollows with strips of smoked salmon.

> Prepare the eggs:

In a small bowl, combine the salt, freshly ground black pepper, and red pepper flakes. Into a separate small bowl, gently crack 1 egg and season with a pinch or two of the salt, pepper, and red chili pepper flake mixture.

Use a spoon to carefully transfer the seasoned yolk into the avocado well trying to keep the yolk intact. If there are any remaining egg whites, add them to the avocado well. Repeat the process with the remaining eggs until all of the avocado halves have been filled.

> Add toppings and bake the avocados:

Top the eggs with red onion. Gently place the sheet pan in the oven and bake the avocados for 15-20 minutes, or until the egg whites have set and the yolks are cooked to your preferred runny-ness.

> Garnish and serve:

Remove avocados from the oven and sprinkle with feta cheese, fresh dill, capers, and everything bagel seasoning. Serve with lemon wedges on the side.

CALORIES: 417

FAT: 29g

CARBS: 30g

PROTEIN: 18g

As it is the most important meal of the day for breaking which follows after a whole day of fasting during Ramadan, it also has a spiritual meaning and significance.

Therefore, the Iftar meal must be as balanced and nutritious as possible. Let's dive in!

1. Mercimek Çorbası (Turkish Lentil Soup)

This comforting and classic Turkish lentil soup recipe features red lentils and spices. Serve bright orange mercimek corbasi with plenty of flavorful garnishes.

PREP TIME: 15 mins

COOK TIME: 35 mins

TOTAL TIME: 50 mins

SERVINGS: 6

Ingredients

- 3 tablespoons olive oil
- 1 large yellow onion, finely diced (about 1 1/4 cups)
- 1 celery rib, finely diced
- 1 carrot, finely diced
- 4 cloves garlic, minced or crushed
- 1 teaspoon ground cumin
- 1 teaspoon dried oregano
- 2 tablespoons tali biber salçasi (Turkish sweet pepper paste)
- 1 1/2 cups (8.8oz/250g) dried red lentils
- 2 liters (8 1/2 cups) vegetable stock
- 1 to 2 lemons, juiced, to taste
- 1 teaspoon salt, or to taste

> 1/2 teaspoon freshly ground black pepper, or to taste

For garnish

> 1/3 cup butter
> 2 teaspoons olive oil
> 2 teaspoons pul biber, plus extra to sprinkle on top
> 6 tablespoons Greek yogurt
> 6 heaping tablespoons croutons
> 1/4 bunch fresh parsley, finely chopped

Directions

> Cook the vegetables:

Heat 3 tablespoons olive oil in a large pot (4 quarts or larger) over medium heat. Add the onion and cook, stirring occasionally, for 3 minutes. Add the celery, carrot, and garlic and sauté until the vegetables soften, about 5 minutes.

> Add the spices and sweet pepper paste:

Add cumin and oregano and stir the spices into the vegetable mixture. Add the tatli biber salçasi and stir until evenly distributed.

> Add the lentils and vegetable stock:

Add the lentils to the pot and stir to distribute evenly into the vegetable mixture. Add the vegetable stock and stir. Let the soup come to a boil.

Turn the heat to low, place the lid on the pot, and let the soup simmer until the lentils and vegetables are tender about 20 minutes.

> Blend the soup and season:

Remove the soup from the heat. Use an immersion blender to purée the soup or work in batches and purée the soup in a blender with the lid cracked.

Add lemon juice, salt, and pepper to taste.

> Prepare the pul biber butter drizzle:

Heat a small saucepan over medium heat and add the butter. Cook the butter until just beginning to turn golden brown, about 3 minutes. Remove from the heat and add 2 teaspoons olive oil and 2 teaspoons pul biber. Stir to combine.

> Garnish and serve soup:

Ladle the soup into bowls. Add 1 tablespoon of Greek yogurt on the top of each soup followed by croutons, a drizzle of the pul biber butter, and a sprinkle of chopped fresh parsley and extra pul biber. Serve.

Leftovers can be stored in an airtight container in the fridge and eaten within 5 days or frozen for up to 3 months.

Reheat the soup in the microwave or a saucepan on low heat.

CALORIES: 343

FAT: 9g

CARBS: 40g

PROTEIN: 9g

2. Whipped Feta with Figs, Pistachio, and Honey

This creamy, salty feta dip with sweet figs, honey, and crunchy pistachios is as pretty as it is tasty. Bring it as a last-minute appetizer to a dinner party or serve it alongside a platter of dips.

PREP TIME: 20 mins

TOTAL TIME: 20 mins

SERVINGS: 4-6

Ingredients

For the fig-pistachio-honey topping

> 2 tablespoons honey, plus more for drizzling
> 1/4 cup roasted and unsalted pistachios, finely chopped
> 1/4 cup finely chopped dried figs
> 2 tablespoons water

For the feta dip

- ➢ 8 ounces feta cheese in brine, drained and crumbled
- ➢ 4 ounces of cream cheese, at room temperature
- ➢ 1/3 cup extra virgin olive oil
- ➢ 1 tablespoon fresh mint leaves, minced
- ➢ 1 small clove of garlic, grated or finely minced
- ➢ 1/8 teaspoon salt
- ➢ 1/4 teaspoon black pepper

For serving

- ➢ Warmed pita bread, naan, or crackers

Directions

- ➢ Make the fig-pistachio-honey topping:

In a small bowl, stir together the honey, pistachios, figs, and water. Place the bowl in a microwave and heat for 30 seconds, just until the mixture begins to bubble. Let cool to room temperature.

Alternatively, you can use the stovetop to make the topping. In a small saucepot over medium heat, combine honey, pistachios, figs, and water. Whisk the ingredients together and cook until the mixture begins to simmer. Remove from the heat and let cool to room temperature.

- ➢ Make the whipped feta:

Into a food processor, add the crumbled feta, cream cheese, olive oil, mint, garlic, salt, and pepper. Pulse for 30 seconds to 1 minute until smooth and creamy (there will still be small bits of feta).

- ➢ Taste and adjust seasoning:

Taste and adjust seasonings with salt and black pepper, if needed. If desired, you can add 2 ounces of cream cheese for a milder flavor.

- ➢ Assemble the dip and serve:

Transfer the feta dip to a wide, shallow serving bowl. Using the back of a spoon, create swoops and swirls in the dip.

Form a divot in the center of the dip and spoon the fig-pistachio-honey topping over the top. Drizzle with additional honey if desired, and serve with warm pita bread, naan, or crackers.

CALORIES: 310

FAT: 27g

CARBS: 13g

PROTEIN: 7g

3. Watermelon Lemonade:

Whole lemons and watermelon are combined to make the most refreshing summer sipper EVER! Watermelon Lemonade is just the right amount of sweet and tart! Perfect and healthy for Iftar after sunset during Ramadan.

PREP TIME: 5 mins

TOTAL TIME: 5 mins

SERVINGS: 4

Ingredients

- ➢ 2 thin-skinned lemons (3 to 3 1/2 ounces each)
- ➢ 4 cups seedless watermelon, rind removed and cubed
- ➢ 1/3 cup sugar
- ➢ 2 cups cold water, divided
- ➢ Ice, for serving

Directions

➢ Wash, trim, and seed lemons:

Wash the lemons to remove any dirt or wax. Trim the hard stem end, cut the lemons into quarters, and remove the seeds. Cut lemon quarters into large chunks.

If your lemon has thicker skin, or if the blossom end is nubby, trim it to reduce bitterness.

➢ Add ingredients into a blender:

Combine the prepared lemons, watermelon, sugar, and 1 cup water in the carafe of a blender.

➢ Blend lemonade:

Blend on high until smooth, about 30 seconds.

➢ Strain the lemonade:

Strain the lemonade over a pitcher using a fine-mesh sieve. Use a silicone spatula to press the pulp against the strainer and wring out the remaining juice. You could discard the pulp if you'd like.

➢ Add the water and serve:

Add the remaining 1 cup water. Stir to combine. Serve lemonade over ice.

CALORIES: 207

FAT: 1g

CARBS: 56g

PROTEIN: 3g

4. Yellow Split Pea Soup:

This bowl of hearty vegan and gluten-free spiced yellow split pea soup is a filling sunset dinner for Iftar during Ramadan. You can top this recipe with yogurt, pepitas, and fresh cilantro, then carry on!

PREP TIME: 15 mins

COOK TIME: 3 hrs

TOTAL TIME: 3 hrs 15 mins

SERVINGS: 6

Ingredients

- 2 tablespoons olive oil
- 1 large onion, finely chopped
- 1 rib celery, finely chopped
- 1 clove garlic, finely chopped
- 1 (1-inch) piece fresh ginger, peeled and finely chopped
- 1/4 teaspoon freshly ground black pepper, or to taste
- 1 jalapeño or other hot pepper, cored, seeded, and finely chopped
- 1 teaspoon ground turmeric
- 1 teaspoon ground cumin
- 1 teaspoon ground coriander
- 1 pound (2 1/4 cups) yellow split peas
- 2 quarts (8 cups) water, or more if needed
- 1 bay leaf
- 1/2 teaspoon kosher salt, or to taste
- Juice of 1/2 lemon (about 4 tablespoons), or more to taste
- 1/2 cup yogurt or sour cream, to serve (omit if making a vegan soup)
- 2 tablespoons chopped fresh cilantro, to serve
- 3 tablespoons roasted, salted pepitas, to serve

Directions

- Sauté the vegetables and seasonings:

In a soup pot over medium heat, warm the oil. When the oil is hot, add the onion, celery, garlic, ginger, and pepper. Sauté, stirring often, for 8 minutes, until the onions are looking translucent and softened.

- Add the hot pepper and spices:

Stir in the jalapeno (or other hot pepper), turmeric, cumin, and coriander. Cook, stirring constantly, for 2 minutes.

➢ Stir in the split peas:

Continue stirring until they are coated with the onion/celery mixture.

➢ Add the water and boil:

Pour in the water and bring to a boil, stirring. Add the bay leaf.

➢ Simmer the soup:

Cover the pot and let the soup bubble gently for 1 1/2 hours, until most of the split peas have fallen apart and are tender.

Stir the soup occasionally. If the soup looks like it has broken down at this point, add the salt, stir, and cook for another 30 minutes until the soup looks thick and creamy, then move on to step 6.

If your split peas still feel firm, cook for an additional 30 to 60 minutes (2 1/2 to 3 hours total cooking time) before adding the salt. Add more water if the soup seems too thick.

➢ Add the lemon juice and taste for seasoning:

Once the split peas are tender, add the lemon juice, plus additional salt and black pepper to taste. Stir to combine.

➢ Serve the soup:

Ladle into bowls and garnish with yogurt or sour cream, cilantro, and pepitas.

CALORIES: 371

FAT: 8g

CARBS: 56g

PROTEIN: 22g

Note: Outdated or expired split peas likely are to be blamed if your split peas aren't softening even after hours of cooking. Who knows how long your split peas have been in a warehouse before they were put on the shelf, even if you just bought them! The best place to get split peas is at a reputable grocery shop where there appears to be a large turnover of beans and legumes. Split peas from these businesses are more likely to be consistently fresh.

Crispy Vegetable Samosa with a bright, spicy cilantro mint dipping sauce is just what your Friday Iftar night needs. The dough, filling, and chutney can be made ahead of time. They are also easy to freeze. Make samosas now, and save some for later during your Ramadan!

PREP TIME: 90 mins

COOK TIME: 30 mins

TOTAL TIME: 2 hrs

SERVINGS: 8-12

Ingredients

For the cilantro mint chutney:

- 2 cups cilantro, coarsely chopped
- 1 cup mint leaves
- 1/4 cup lemon juice, from about 1 large lemon
- 4 to 5 cloves garlic
- 1 to 1 1/2 jalapenos, chopped
- 1 (1-inch) gingerroot, peeled and chopped
- 1 1/2 teaspoons salt
- 1 1/2 teaspoons cumin seeds

For the dough:

- 1 cup all-purpose flour
- 1 teaspoon salt
- 2 tablespoons melted ghee or vegetable oil
- 1/4 cup cold water, added a tablespoon at a time

For the filling:

- 2 medium russet potatoes, peeled, quartered
- 1 tablespoon oil, plus more to wrap the samosas

- ➢ 1/2 teaspoon cumin seeds
- ➢ 1 medium onion, chopped
- ➢ 1 1/2 teaspoons minced jalapeno
- ➢ 1 teaspoon ground coriander
- ➢ 1/2 teaspoon garam masala
- ➢ 1/2 teaspoon ground turmeric
- ➢ 1 teaspoon salt
- ➢ 1/2 cup green peas, frozen and thawed

For frying:

- ➢ 2 1/2 cups vegetable oil

Directions

- ➢ Make the chutney:

Combine cilantro, mint, lemon juice, garlic cloves, jalapeños, ginger root, salt, and cumin seeds in a blender or food processor. It should be thick enough to coat a samosa when dipped.

If you want it thinner, add 2 to 3 tablespoons of water. Transfer the chutney to a bowl, cover it, and wait until the samosas are ready.

- ➢ Begin making the samosa dough:

In a large mixing bowl, combine all-purpose flour and salt.

- ➢ Drizzle in the ghee:

Drizzle the melted ghee or vegetable oil around the flour mixture. Pick up a handful of the dough and rub it between your palms to mix the ghee as evenly into the flour as possible.

- ➢ Check the ratio of flour to ghee:

To see if the flour-to-ghee ratio is good enough to make crispy pastry, hold a portion of the mixture in your hand and make a tight fist, then open it. The mixture should hold its shape.

- ➢ Add water:

Add water to the flour one to two tablespoons at a time while kneading. Knead into a smooth, firm dough. This should take about 5 minutes. Wrap the dough in cling wrap or cover it with a damp cloth until ready to fill the samosas.

> ➤ Make the filling:

Set a medium pot filled with water over medium-high heat. Add the peeled quartered potatoes, and bring them to a boil. Boil the potatoes until they are forking tender, about 15 minutes.

Set a large skillet over medium-high heat and add the oil. Once the oil shimmers, add the cumin seeds to the skillet. Once they sputter, turn the heat down to medium and add the onion. Sauté for 3-4 minutes until the onion is softened. Add jalapeno, coriander, garam masala, ground turmeric, and salt. Give it a quick stir. Add the peas.

Drain the potatoes and add them to the skillet. Using the back of a wooden spoon or a potato masher, coarsely mash the mixture, leaving no large chunks of potatoes. Stir to combine. You want it mixed well. In the end, the filling should be relatively dry and thick.

Set aside to cool completely before filling the samosas.

> ➤ Knead the dough:

While the filling is cooling, unwrap the dough, and knead it again for a couple minutes to make it smooth.

> ➤ Divide and shape the dough:

Divide into 6 equal parts. Roll each into smooth balls, and cover with a damp cloth. Pick one ball, press it between your palms to flatten, and lightly dab the surface of the dough with oil or ghee. This prevents the rolling pin from sticking to the dough. Resist the urge to dust the countertop with flour, as the loose flour will burn when you drop the dough in the oil to fry, giving the samosa an off-taste.

Use a rolling pin to flatten the dough into a circle 6 inches in diameter, 1 mm in thickness. Cut in half so you have two half-moon shapes.

If you're having a difficult time rolling out the dough, place the round between pieces of wax paper or parchment.

> ➤ Fill the samosa:

Pick one half and brush the edges with water using your finger.

Pick one edge of the dough and place it on top of the other edge, making a cone shape. Gently pinch along the edges of the cone, making sure they are sealed.

Add 1 1/2 tablespoons of filling into the cone. This should fill it 3/4 of the way. Brush water on the edges of the cone's opening, and pinch the edges together to close the samosa.

Repeat with the rest of the dough. Cover sealed samosas with a damp cloth. In the end, you should have 12 samosas.

➢ Fry the samosas:

In a deep pot, add the oil and heat to 200°F over medium heat. Add the samosas to the oil and fry in batches; do not overcrowd the pot. Fry until the samosas begin to turn golden.

Once the samosas are golden, increase the heat to medium-high, bringing the temperature up to 350°F, and cook for another 5 minutes until the samosas have darkened to a deeper brown.

Take the samosas out of the oil and transfer them to a plate lined with paper towels.

Reduce the heat back to medium or medium-low, until the oil temperature drops back to 200°F before going forward with the next batch of samosas. Getting this part right for a samosa is the trickiest part. If you start with high-temperature oil, the pastry will turn soggy and oily. So, starting with warm oil and then increasing the heat is the way to go here.

➢ Serve:

Serve immediately with a side of green cilantro mint chutney.

CALORIES: 113

FAT: 4g

CARBS: 18g

PROTEIN: 3g

6. Lentil Soup:

Three things make this vegetarian lentil soup so good which are; caramelized onions, toasted tomato paste (it's very easy!), and lots of carrots and celery. Make use of a big pot to have some now and save some for later for Iftar during your Ramadan journey, this soup is freezer-friendly!

PREP TIME: 15 mins

COOK TIME: 1 hr

TOTAL TIME: 1 hr 15 mins

SERVINGS: 6-8

Ingredients

- 2 tablespoons olive oil
- 1 large yellow onion, finely diced
- 2 tablespoons tomato paste
- 1 teaspoon dried thyme
- 1 clove garlic, finely diced
- 3 stalks celery, finely diced
- 3 carrots, peeled and finely diced
- 2 cups (12 ounces) small green French lentils
- 8 cups water or vegetable stock
- 1 tablespoon low-sodium soy sauce
- 1 1/2 teaspoons kosher salt, plus more to taste
- 1/8 teaspoon freshly ground black pepper, plus more to taste
- 3 tablespoons lemon juice, plus more to taste
- 1/2 bunch of kale, stemmed and thinly sliced crosswise

Directions

- Caramelize the onions:

In a soup pot over medium heat, heat the olive oil. Once the oil shimmers, add the onions and cook, stirring occasionally for 10 minutes, or until deep, golden brown.

▷ Cook the tomato paste and vegetables:

Push the onions to the side of the pot. And in the space you made, add the tomato paste. Stir for 2 to 3 minutes, or until the tomato paste darkens to a ruddy brown. Add the thyme, garlic, celery, and carrots. Cook and stir for 2 minutes.

▷ Add the lentils and liquid, then simmer:

Add the lentils, 8 cups water, soy sauce, salt, and pepper to the pot. Adjust the heat to medium, so the soup is just at a gentle simmer. Simmer for 55 to 60 minutes, or until the lentils are soft.

▷ Finish the soup and serve:

Scoop out 2 cups of the soup and purée it in a blender until smooth, or use an immersion blender and purée just until the soup takes on a little body and thickens, but you still have texture. Return the blended soup to the pot and stir in the lemon juice. Add the sliced kale and simmer until the kale softens about 1 to 2 minutes.

Taste, and add more salt, pepper, and lemon juice, if you like. Serve with a nice slice of crusty bread or a side salad.

CALORIES: 240

FAT: 4g

CARBS: 39g

PROTEIN: 13g

7. Olive Crostini:

The perfect easy and quick appetizer, tasty and fun to make during this Ramadan period.

PREP TIME: 15 mins

COOK TIME: 2 mins

TOTAL TIME: 17 mins

SERVINGS: 24 toasts

Note: You'll need a food processor for this

Ingredients

- 1/2 cup black olives, pitted
- 1/2 cup green olives with pimientos
- 2 medium cloves garlic
- 1/2 cup grated Parmesan cheese
- 2 tablespoons extra virgin olive oil
- 4 tablespoons butter
- 1/2 cup Monterey jack cheese
- 1/4 cup parsley, chopped
- 1 baguette

Directions

- Make olive mixture:

Chop the olives in a food processor. Transfer to a medium bowl. With the machine running, drop garlic through the feed tube of the food processor and mince.

Add Parmesan, butter, and olive oil, and process into a paste. Add butter mixture to bowl with olives. Fold in jack cheese and parsley.

- Cut the baguette into thin slices and top with olive mixture:

Spread each slice generously with olive mixture.

- Broil:

Cook under broiler until bubbly and lightly browned - about 2 minutes.

Serve right out of the oven. Helps to make the olive mixture in advance and spread right before you put it in the oven.

CALORIES: 129

FAT: 6g

CARBS: 15g

PROTEIN: 4g

8. Mediterranean Mezze Platter:

It's easy enough for an Iftar night dinner, but festive enough to serve special guests during this Ramadan period. You'll be wondering right? Dig in and see…

PREP TIME: 20 mins

TOTAL TIME: 20 mins

SERVINGS: 4

Ingredients

- 1/2 cup Kalamata or other flavorful olives
- 1/2 cup plain Greek yogurt, stirred with a pinch of salt and drizzle of olive oil
- 1 cup hummus (homemade or store-bought)
- 1 cup Easy Muhammara
- 2/3 English cucumber, sliced
- 1 cup cherry tomatoes
- 1 large carrot, cut on the diagonal into slices
- Small bunch grapes
- 4 ounces feta cheese, broken into pieces, lightly drizzled with olive oil and a pinch of herbs
- 3 pita breads, quartered, brushed lightly with olive oil, and warmed in the oven

Directions

- Assemble the mezze platter:

Set out a large platter or generous cutting board. Put the olives, yogurt, hummus, and muhammara in small dishes and add to the platter. Arrange the cucumber, tomatoes, carrots, grapes, and feta on the platter. Fill in with the warm pita just before serving.

CALORIES: 611

FAT: 35g

CARBS: 58g

PROTEIN: 23g

Note: Scale the amounts up or down based on how many are seated at your table; use the ingredients mentioned as a starting point with leeway to substitute different dips, veggies, or fruits depending on what's in season and what you have on hand.

9. Grilled Tuna Kebabs:

Get your grill on with tuna kabobs! skewers of marinated fresh tuna, onions, bell peppers, and mushrooms.

PREP TIME: 20 mins

COOK TIME: 15 mins

MARINATING: 60 mins

TOTAL TIME: 90 mins

SERVINGS: 4

Ingredients

- ➢ 1 1/2 pounds tuna, swordfish or sturgeon steaks
- ➢ 1 red bell pepper
- ➢ 1 green bell pepper
- ➢ 1 small onion (sweet if available)

> 6 to 10 large button mushrooms
> 2 lemons, cut into wedges

Marinade Ingredients

> 1/2 cup extra virgin olive oil
> 2 tablespoons onion, chopped
> 1 tablespoon fresh rosemary, chopped
> 1 teaspoon salt
> 1/2 teaspoon black pepper
> 2 cloves garlic

Special Equipment

> Food Processor

Directions

> Cut into bite-sized pieces:

Cut all the fish and veggies into similar-sized pieces; this helps everything lay flat when it is on the grill.

> Marinate the fish and vegetables:

To make the marinade, purée the onion, rosemary, garlic, salt and pepper in a food processor. Drizzle in the olive oil while puréeing, continue to purée until smooth, about 1-2 minutes.

Coat the fish and veggies in the marinade. Set in the fridge for at least an hour and up to overnight.

> Thread onto skewers:

When skewering the fish and vegetables, pierce the fish against the grain, and select pieces of veggies that are close to the same size as your fish. This is important because if the pieces are different widths, some things will be charred and others undercooked.

You also want to be careful when loading up the skewers; it's easy to stab yourself by accident!

Alternate pieces of fish with pieces of various veggies, leaving a little space between everything. Don't crowd the skewer, or the parts that are touching will cook too slowly.

Note that by threading the skewers with assorted veggies and fish, some things will be cooked more or less than others, as some things take longer to cook than others.

If you want all of your items to be cooked perfectly, use a separate skewer for the onions, one for the tuna, one for the bell peppers, etc. Put the onions and bell peppers down first because they take longer to cook.

➢ Grill on high, direct heat:

Prepare the grill for high, direct heat. Clean the grates and wipe them down with a paper towel that has been dipped in vegetable oil. Lay the skewers on the grill.

Don't move them until the fish pieces are well browned on one side, about 3-6 minutes.

Then using tongs, carefully turn the skewers over and cook them until they are seared on the other side.

Serve hot or at room temperature. Drizzle with lemon juice or serve with lemon wedges.

CALORIES: 376

FAT: 8g

CARBS: 36g

PROTEIN: 45g

Note: Either single or double skewers can be used. Although single skewers are simpler to load, turning them becomes more challenging as the food revolves around them. Although loading double skewers is a little more difficult, the food remains on them   better.
To help keep bamboo skewers from catching fire on a hot grill, soak them in water for   at   least   an   hour   before   grilling.

If you use vinegar or lemon in the marinade, the fish will get overcooked.

10. Jeweled Rice Salad:

Perfect for your next weekend or Iftar cooking plan, this vibrant, fragrant version of Persian Jeweled Rice Salad features butternut squash, toasted pistachios and almonds, warm spices, and tender dried fruit!

PREP TIME: 20 mins

COOK TIME: 45 mins

TOTAL TIME: 65 mins

SERVINGS: 6-8

Ingredients

For the salad:

- 1 1/2 cups wild rice
- 8 cups water
- 1 1/4 teaspoons salt, divided
- 1 half butternut squash, peeled (about 1 pound), cut into 3/4-inch cubes
- 3 tablespoons Filippo Berio Delicato extra virgin olive oil, divided
- 1/8 teaspoon ground black pepper
- 1/3 cup blanched slivered almonds
- 1/3 cup shelled pistachios
- 1/2 red onion, finely chopped
- 1/2 teaspoon ground cinnamon
- 1/2 teaspoon ground coriander seed
- 1/2 teaspoon ground turmeric
- 1/8 teaspoon ground cloves
- 1/3 cup dried cranberries
- 1/3 cup golden raisins
- 1/3 cup apricots, finely diced
- Finely grated zest from 1 orange
- 1/2 cup pomegranate seeds (from about 1/2 pomegranate)
- 1 handful torn mint leaves

For the dressing:

> - 1/3 cup freshly squeezed orange juice
> - 2 tablespoons white wine vinegar
> - 1 teaspoon honey
> - 1/4 teaspoon salt
> - 1/8 teaspoon ground black pepper
> - 1/3 cup Filippo Berio Delicato extra virgin olive oil

Directions

> - Cook the rice:

In a large pot, bring 8 cups water and 1 teaspoon of the salt to a boil. Add the rice, return the water to a boil, and immediately reduce the heat to a gentle simmer. Simmer for 45 minutes, or until the rice is tender.

Drain in a sieve or fine-mesh colander. Transfer to a large bowl.

> - Roast the squash:

Preheat the oven to 450oF. On a rimmed baking sheet, mound the squash in the center. Sprinkle with 2 tablespoons of olive oil, remaining 1/4 teaspoon salt, and pepper. Toss to coat the squash, massaging the olive oil into the cubes to coat them.

Spread in one layer and roast for 20 to 25 minutes, or until tender. Remove and cool on the baking sheet.

> - Toast the nuts:

In a medium skillet over medium heat, toast the almonds and pistachios until the almonds are golden and the nuts are fragrant about 4 minutes. Transfer to a plate.

> - Cook the onions and bloom the spices:

Add the remaining 1 tablespoon olive oil to the skillet. Over medium heat, cook the onions, stirring occasionally, for 4 to 5 minutes or until softened. Add the ground cinnamon, ground coriander, turmeric, and ground cloves. Stir for 30 seconds.

Fold in the cranberries, raisins, and apricots and remove from heat.

> - Make the dressing:

In a small bowl, combine the orange juice, vinegar, honey, salt, and pepper. Whisk in the olive oil until emulsified. Taste and add more salt or pepper, as desired.

> ➢ Assemble the salad:

Add the squash, toasted nuts, onions, spices, dried fruits, and orange zest to the bowl of rice. Toss with half the dressing (you will have more than you need). Taste and add more salt, pepper, or dressing as desired.

> ➢ Serve:

Mound the rice on a platter or in a serving bowl, and garnish with the pomegranate seeds and mint leaves. Serve at room temperature.

CALORIES: 325

FAT: 19g

CARBS: 38g

PROTEIN: 5g

11. Cucumber Lime Mint Agua Fresca:

Cucumber Mint Agua Fresca! So cool and refreshing made with cucumbers, lime, and mint. Perfect way to cool down after fasting on a hot day!

PREP TIME: 15 mins

TOTAL TIME: 15 mins

SERVINGS: 4

Ingredients

> ➢ 1-pound cucumbers (about 2 good-sized cucumbers), ends trimmed but peel still on, coarsely chopped
> ➢ 1/2 cup lime juice from fresh limes (from about 1 pound of limes, or 5 to 10 limes, depending on how juicy they are)

- ➢ 1 1/4 cups packed (spearmint) mint leaves (about a large handful), woody stems removed
- ➢ 1/2 cup sugar
- ➢ Approximately 1 1/4 cups water

Directions

- ➢ Blend ingredients:

Put ingredients in blender, add enough water to fill 3/4 of blender. Hold the lid on the blender and purée until smooth.

- ➢ Strain out solids:

Place a fine mesh sieve over a bowl and pour the purée through it, pressing against the sieve with a rubber spatula or the back of a spoon to extract as much liquid out as possible.

- ➢ Add ice:

Fill a large pitcher halfway with ice cubes. Add the juice. Serve with sprigs of mint and slices of lime.

CALORIES: 125

FAT: 0g

CARBS: 32g

PROTEIN: 1g

12. Air Fryer Falafel:

Falafel made in the air fryer is crunchy on the outside and soft in the middle. Stuff them in a pita packed with veggies and tahini sauce for an easy, quick Iftar Ramadan meal!

PREP TIME: 10 mins

COOK TIME: 14 mins

TOTAL TIME: 24 mins

SERVINGS: 6

YIELD: 25-30 Falafel

Ingredients

For the tahini sauce:

- 1/2 cup tahini
- 1/4 cup Greek yogurt
- 1/2 lemon, juice only
- 2 tablespoons olive oil
- 1/4 to 1/2 cup hot water

For the falafel:

- 2 (15-ounce) cans chickpeas, rinsed and drained
- 1/4 cup fresh parsley
- 1/4 cup cilantro
- 2 cloves garlic
- 1 large shallot, chopped
- 3 tablespoons all-purpose flour
- 2 tablespoons sesame seeds
- 2 teaspoons ground cumin
- 1 teaspoon paprika
- 1/2 lemon, juice only
- 1 teaspoon salt
- Spray olive oil, for cooking

For serving:

- 6 pita breads
- Fresh lettuce
- 1 large tomato, sliced thinly
- 1/2 red onion, sliced thinly
- 1 cucumber, sliced thinly

Special Equipment

> Food Processor

Directions

> Make the tahini sauce:

In a medium bowl, stir together tahini, yogurt, lemon juice, and olive oil. The mixture will be very thick to start. Thin it out with hot water until it's easily spreadable. You'll have to slowly add 1/4 to 1/2 cup of hot water to get it to the right consistency.

> Make the falafel mixture:

In the bowl of a food processor, add the chickpeas, parsley, cilantro, garlic, shallot, flour, sesame seeds, cumin, paprika, lemon, and salt. Pulse until the mixture comes together in a rough paste. It shouldn't be completely smooth.

Shape the falafel mixture into tablespoon-sized discs, about 1-inch in diameter. Repeat until you use all the falafel mixture. You should get 25 to 30 falafel discs.

> Air fry the falafel:

Spray the basket for your air fryer with some nonstick olive oil. Add as many falafel discs into the basket as you can without them touching and spray them with olive oil very lightly. Air fry the falafel at 350°F° for 8 minutes. Flip and fry for another 6 minutes on the second side.

Repeat until you've cooked all the falafel.

> Serve the falafel:

Serve the falafel in warm pita (I like to microwave my pita first for 15 seconds). Serve with tahini yogurt sauce and any toppings you like!

Leftover falafel will store great in the fridge for 5 to 6 days or you can freeze the falafel for longer storage. Reheat falafel in a 350°F oven for 10 to 12 minutes until warmed through.

CALORIES: 553

FAT: 21g

CARBS: 76g

PROTEIN: 19g

Note: **Alternative cooking options: If you don't have an air fryer, you can do one of these two things:**

Deep frying: If deep frying, then, roll them into balls rather than discs. Deep fry them at 350°F for about 4 minutes until they are golden brown on the outside.

Frying on a Pan: This works best in a cast iron skillet with about 1 inch of oil in the skillet. If you are using the pan fry method, shape the falafel into discs, like that of air frying. Fry the falafel over medium-high heat for 3 to 4 minutes per side. Done!

Remove and drain on paper towels.

13. Quick Easy Fish Stew:

Make this delicious fish stew with just a handful of ingredients in 30 minutes.

PREP TIME: 15 mins

COOK TIME: 19 mins

TOTAL TIME: 34 mins

SERVINGS: 4

Ingredients

- 6 tablespoons extra virgin olive oil
- 1 medium onion, chopped (about 1 1/2 cups)
- 3 large cloves garlic, minced
- 2/3 cup fresh parsley leaves, chopped
- 1 1/2 cups fresh chopped tomato OR 1 (14-ounce) can whole or crushed tomatoes with their juices
- 2 teaspoons tomato paste, optional
- 1 (8-ounce) bottle clam juice (or 1 cup **shellfish stock**)
- 1/2 cup dry white wine (such as Sauvignon blanc)

- ➢ 1 1/2 pounds firm white fish fillets such as halibut, cod, red snapper, or sea bass, cut into 2-inch pieces
- ➢ Pinch dried oregano
- ➢ Pinch dried thyme
- ➢ 1/8 teaspoon Tabasco sauce , or more to taste
- ➢ 1/8 teaspoon freshly ground black pepper, plus more to taste
- ➢ 1 teaspoon salt, plus more to taste

Directions

- ➢ Saute the aromatics in olive oil:

Heat olive oil in a large, thick-bottomed pot over medium-high heat. Add onion and sauté 4 minutes. Add the garlic and cook a minute more. Add parsley and stir 2 minutes. Add tomato and tomato paste, and gently cook for 10 more minutes or so.

- ➢ Finish the soup:

Add clam juice, dry white wine, and fish. Bring to a simmer, and let simmer until the fish is cooked through and easily flakes apart, about 3 to 5 minutes. Add seasoning—salt, pepper, oregano, thyme, and Tabasco. Add more salt and pepper to taste.

- ➢ Serve the stew:

Ladle into individual bowls and serve.

Great served with crusty bread for dipping in the fish stew broth.

CALORIES: 389

FAT: 3g

CARBS: 7g

PROTEIN: 33g

Note: You can add 1/2 pound of shrimp, mussels, clams, or scallops to the stew as an alternative. If you plan to add shellfish, do so a few minutes ahead of the fish as they   require   extra   time   to   cook   and   open. You may use one cup of shellfish stock in place of the clam juice.

14. Chicken Mulligatawny Soup:

This mulligatawny is more than soup—it's the ultimate one-bowl meal perfect for your Ramadan Iftar meal.

PREP TIME: 15 mins

COOK TIME: 50 mins

TOTAL TIME: 65 mins

SERVINGS: 4-6

Ingredients

- 2 tablespoons butter
- 1 tablespoon extra virgin olive oil
- 1 large onion, chopped (about 2 cups)
- 2 ribs celery, chopped (about 1 cup)
- 2 carrots, chopped (about 1 cup)
- 2 bay leaves
- 4 teaspoons curry powder
- 1 1/4 pound (570g) boneless, skinless chicken thighs, trimmed of visible fat
- 2 cups (475 ml) chicken stock
- 2 cups (475 ml) water
- 1 1/2 teaspoons kosher salt (or 1 teaspoon sea salt)
- 1/4 cup uncooked basmati rice
- 2 tart apples, cored, peeled, and chopped (about 2 cups)
- 1/4 cup (60 ml) heavy whipping cream
- 1/4 cup (60 ml) plain yogurt, for garnish
- 1 tablespoon minced chives, for garnish

Directions

➢ Sauté the aromatics:

Heat butter and olive oil on medium high heat in a large (4 to 5 quart), thick-bottomed pot. Add the onions, celery, and carrots. Cook for 5 minutes until just starting to soften. Add the bay leaves. Add the curry powder and mix to coat.

➢ Add the chicken, stock, and salt:

Add the chicken thighs and stir to coat with the curry mixture. Add the stock and water to the pot. Add the salt. Bring to a simmer and reduce the heat to maintain a simmer. Cover and cook for 20 minutes.

➢ Remove the chicken, let cool to touch:

Remove the chicken pieces from the pot. (They should be just cooked through. If not, return them to the pot for another 5 minutes or so, until they are cooked through.) Place on a cutting board and allow to cool to the touch.

➢ Add the rice and apples:

Add the rice and the chopped apples to the soup. Return to a simmer on high heat, then lower the heat to maintain a low simmer. Cover and cook for 15 minutes, or until the rice is cooked through.

➢ Shred the chicken, return it to the soup, and add cream:

While the apples and rice are cooking in the soup, shred the chicken, discarding any tough bits. Once the rice and apples in the soup are cooked, add the chicken back to the pot. Heat for 5 minutes more. Then stir in the cream.

➢ Serve:

Serve with yogurt and chives.

CALORIES: 356

FAT: 18g

CARBS: 24g

PROTEIN: 26g

Note: The recipe calls for tart apples. Try these varieties: Granny Smith, Cripps Pink, Winesap, Braeburn, or Courtland.

15. Asparagus Pakoras with Lemony Yogurt Sauce:

These are crispy fried fritters made with chickpea flour, asparagus, and lots of fresh herbs. It's the perfect comfort food to break the fast during Ramadan.

PREP TIME: 20 mins

COOK TIME: 20 mins

TOTAL TIME: 40 mins

SERVINGS: 4-6

Ingredients

For the yogurt sauce:

- 1 cup full-fat Greek yogurt
- 2 tablespoons fresh lemon juice
- 2 teaspoons lemon zest
- 1/2 teaspoon fresh garlic, finely minced
- 1 teaspoon sea salt

For the pakoras:

- 2 cups (200g) chickpea flour
- 1 pound asparagus (medium thickness), woody ends trimmed and cut into 1/4-inch pieces
- 3 green onions, white and pale green parts only, very thinly sliced lengthwise
- 1/4 cup fresh cilantro leaves and tender stems, coarsely chopped
- 1/4 cup fresh dill, coarsely chopped
- 1 teaspoon sea salt, plus more to taste
- 1 teaspoon cumin seeds
- 1/2 teaspoon cayenne pepper

➢ 1/2 teaspoon baking powder
➢ 1 1/4 cups ice cold water
➢ Vegetable oil, for frying

Directions

➢ Prepare the lemony yogurt sauce:

In a small bowl, whisk together the yogurt, lemon juice, lemon zest, garlic, and salt. Chill in the fridge until ready to serve.

➢ Make the batter:

In a large bowl, add the chickpea flour, asparagus, green onions, cilantro, dill, salt, cumin seeds, cayenne pepper, and baking powder. Use a rubber spatula to stir well until combined. Gradually add the water as you stir to create a smooth, lump-free batter thick enough to coat the spatula.

➢ Prepare to fry the pakoras:

Line a large platter with paper towels and set it aside. You will use it to drain the pakoras.

In a large 10-inch skillet set over medium-high heat, add enough oil to come 1/2 inch up the sides. Heat the oil to 350°F. If you don't have a deep-fry thermometer to check the temperature, test the oil by carefully dropping in a tiny bit of batter. It should bubble up and sizzle.

➢ Fry the pakoras:

To test the batter for seasoning, drop a teaspoon of batter into the oil and fry until golden brown. Cool it slightly on the paper towel-lined platter, then taste. Add more salt to the batter, if needed.

Working in batches, carefully add 2-tablespoon dollops of batter into the oil, leaving about 1/2 inch between each. Use the back of the spoon to lightly tap the tops to flatten.

Fry them for 1 minute to 1 minute 30 seconds per side, until they turn golden brown and are cooked through. Adjust the heat up or down, as necessary, to maintain a temperature of 350°F to 360°F. Transfer the fried pakoras onto the prepared platter to drain.

Repeat with remaining batter.

> Serve:

Enjoy the pakoras warm with the lemony yogurt on the side for dipping.

Leftovers store well in the fridge for up to 5 days. To warm them up, I would suggest placing them on a sheet pan in the oven for 7 to 10 minutes at 300°F. You can also use a toaster oven on the 'toast' setting.

CALORIES: 209

FAT: 7g

CARBS: 25g

PROTEIN: 13g

BON APPETIT!

I hope these recipes inspire you and as well serve as your companion throughout your Ramadan journey. May your culinary journey with these Ramadan recipes be both a gastronomic delight and a transformative pathway to a healthier, more vibrant you.

HERE IS YOUR BONUS

28-Day Ramadan Meal Table Planner

DAYS	SUHOOR	IFTAR

DAYS	SUHOOR	IFTAR

DAYS	SUHOOR	IFTAR

DAYS	SUHOOR	IFTAR

Have a blessed month of Ramadan!!!

As we come to the close of this Ramadan recipe book, I want to thank you once again for choosing it as your companion on this holy journey.

Ramadan is a time for reflection, compassion, and community. I hope this book has, in some way, helped you connect with the spirit of the season.

Whether you're a seasoned cook or just starting to explore the world of Ramadan cuisine, I wish you a blessed and fulfilling Ramadan filled with delicious food, shared laughter, and spiritual growth.

From the bottom of my heart, jazakallahu khairan (may God reward you) for your support.

May peace and blessings be with you always.

Warmly,

Melvin A. Orr

www.ingramcontent.com/pod-product-compliance
Lightning Source LLC
Chambersburg PA
CBHW060518120726
48002CB00011B/3226